READING POWER

Nature's Greatest Hits

THE SAHARA
World's Largest Desert

Jil Fine

The Rosen Publishing Group's
PowerKids Press™
New York

Published in 2002 by The Rosen Publishing Group, Inc.
29 East 21st Street, New York, NY 10010

First Edition

Book Design: Michael DeLisio

Photo Credits: Cover © Indexstock; pp. 4-5 © Tiziana and Gianni Baldizzone/Corbis; p. 8 © Craig Aurness/Corbis; pp. 10-11 © Wolfgang Kaehler/Corbis; p.12 © Corbis; p. 13 © FPG; pp. 14-15 © Indexstock; p. 15 © Neil Rabinowitz/Corbis; pp. 16-17 © Jamie Harron; Papilio/Corbis; pp. 18-19 © Inge Yspeert/Corbis; p. 19 © Charles & Rosette Lenars/Corbis; p. 20 © Peter Arnold Inc.; p. 21 © Yann Arthur-Bertrand/Corbis

Fine, Jill.
The Sahara : world's largest desert / by Jil Fine.
p. cm. - (Nature's greatest hits)
Includes bibliographical references (p.).
ISBN 0-8239-6013-7 (lib. bdg.)
1. Sahara-Juvenile literature. [1. Sahara.] I. Title. II. Series.
DT334 .F56 2001
916.602-dc21

00-013250

Manufactured in the United States of America

Contents

World's Largest Desert

The Sahara desert is the largest desert in the world. There is sand and rock as far as the eye can see.

FUN FACT: The word *sahara* means "desert" in the Arabic language.

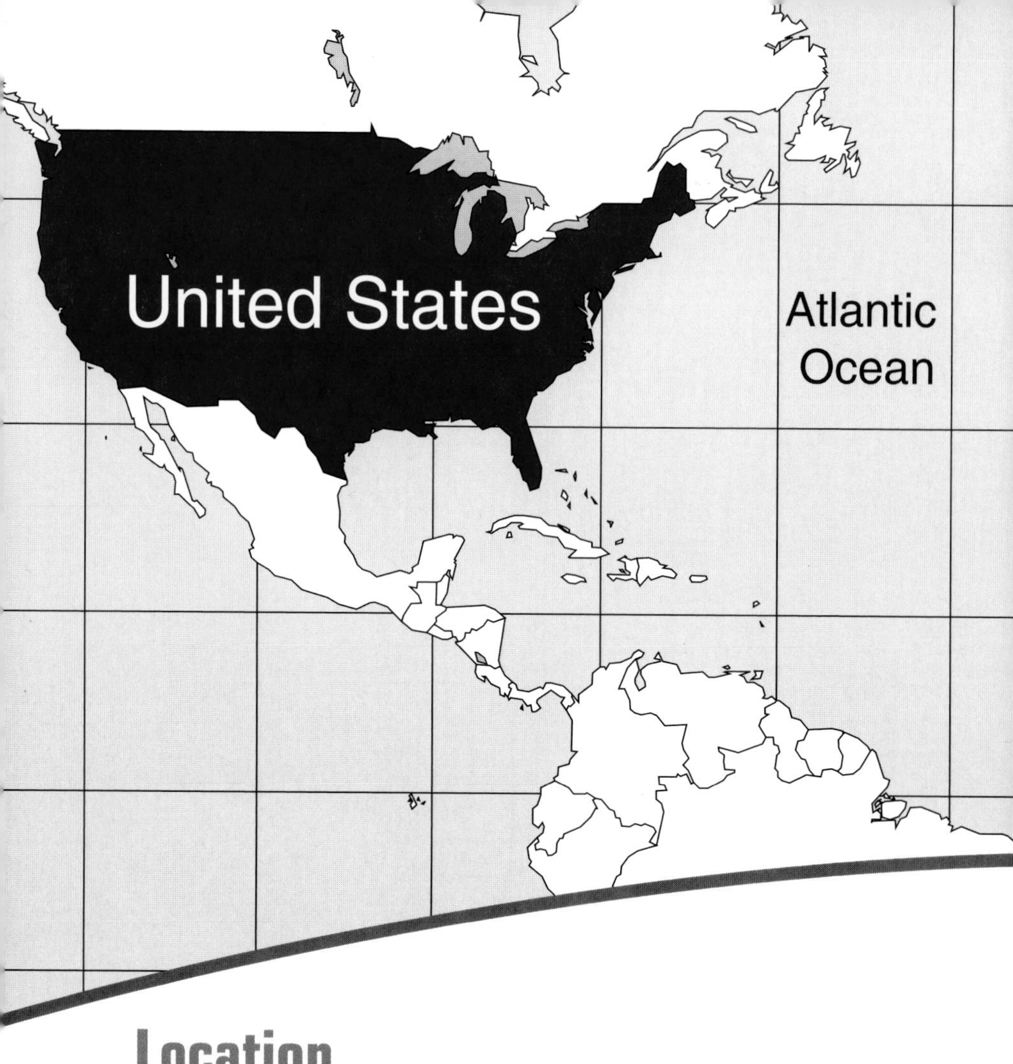

Location

The Sahara desert is in Africa. It is 3.32 million square miles. It is more than two times the size of any other desert in the world. It is almost the same size as the United States!

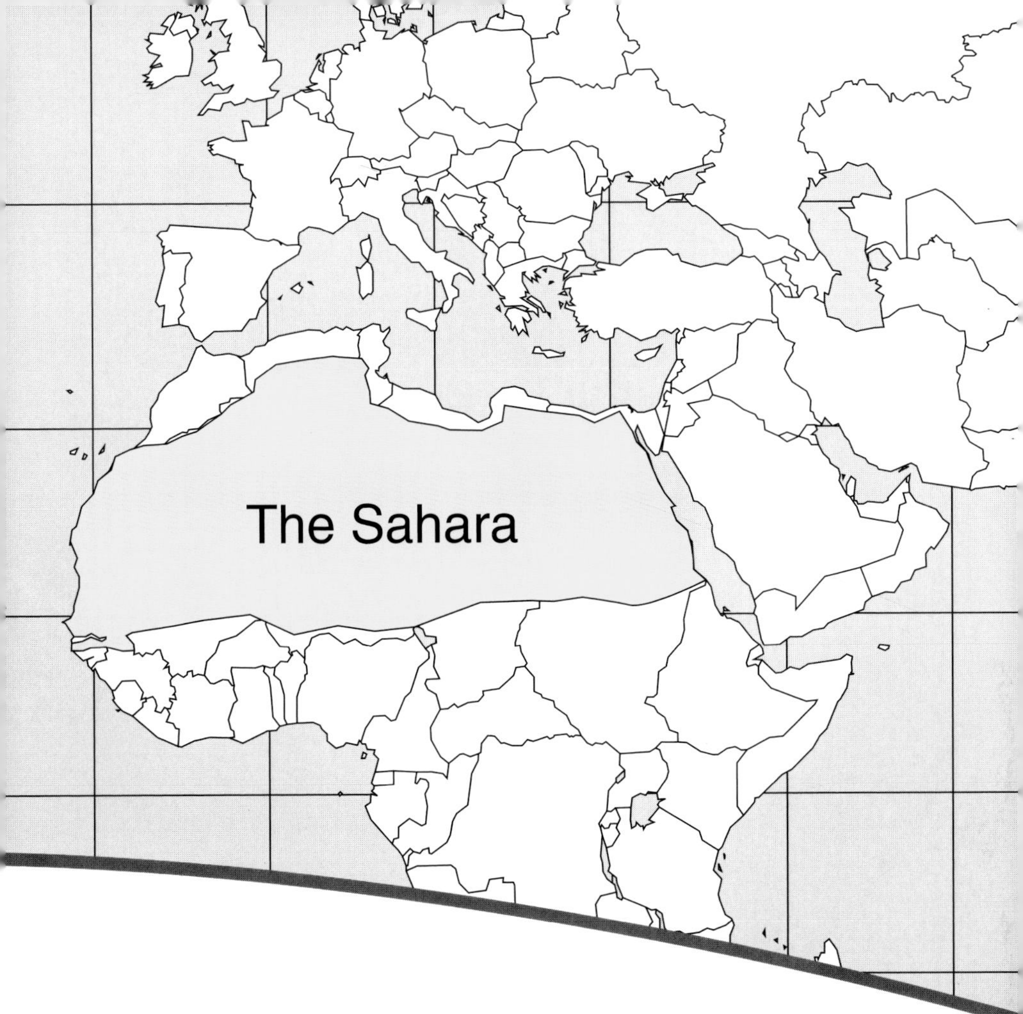

The Three Largest Deserts	
Sahara	3.32 million square miles
Australian	1.47 million square miles
Arabian	0.5 million square miles

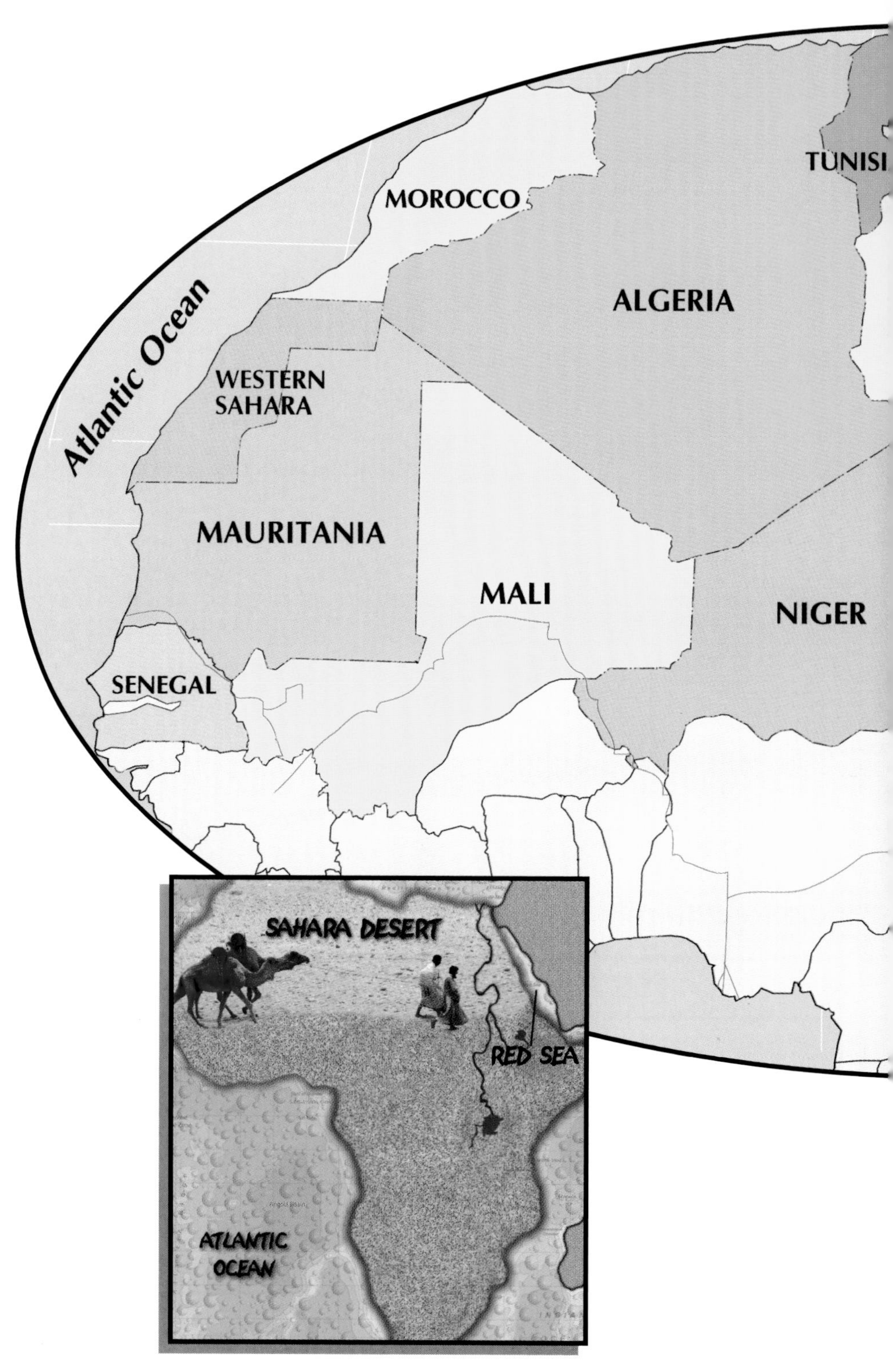

TUNISI
MOROCCO
ALGERIA
Atlantic Ocean
WESTERN
SAHARA
MAURITANIA
MALI
NIGER
SENEGAL
SAHARA DESERT
RED SEA
ATLANTIC
OCEAN

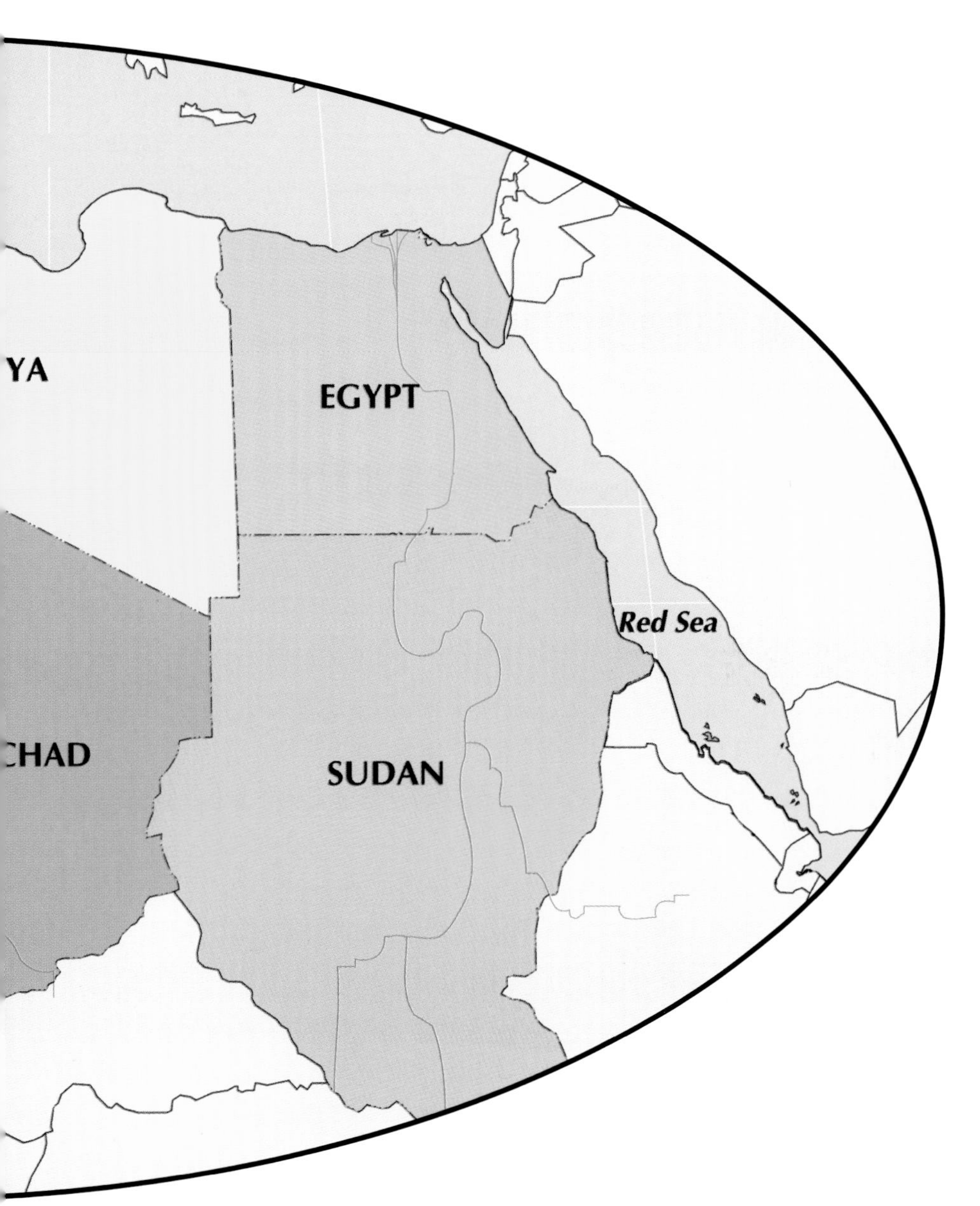

The Sahara goes from the Atlantic Ocean in the west to the Red Sea in the east. It runs through 12 countries.

Climate

The Sahara desert is very hot and dry. It almost never rains. In some parts, less than three inches of rain fall in a year!

FUN FACT: In the Sahara, you need to drink water every four hours to stay alive.

In the day, the temperature can be 130 degrees Fahrenheit.

FUN FACT: One day in 1922, the temperature in the Sahara hit 136 degrees Fahrenheit.

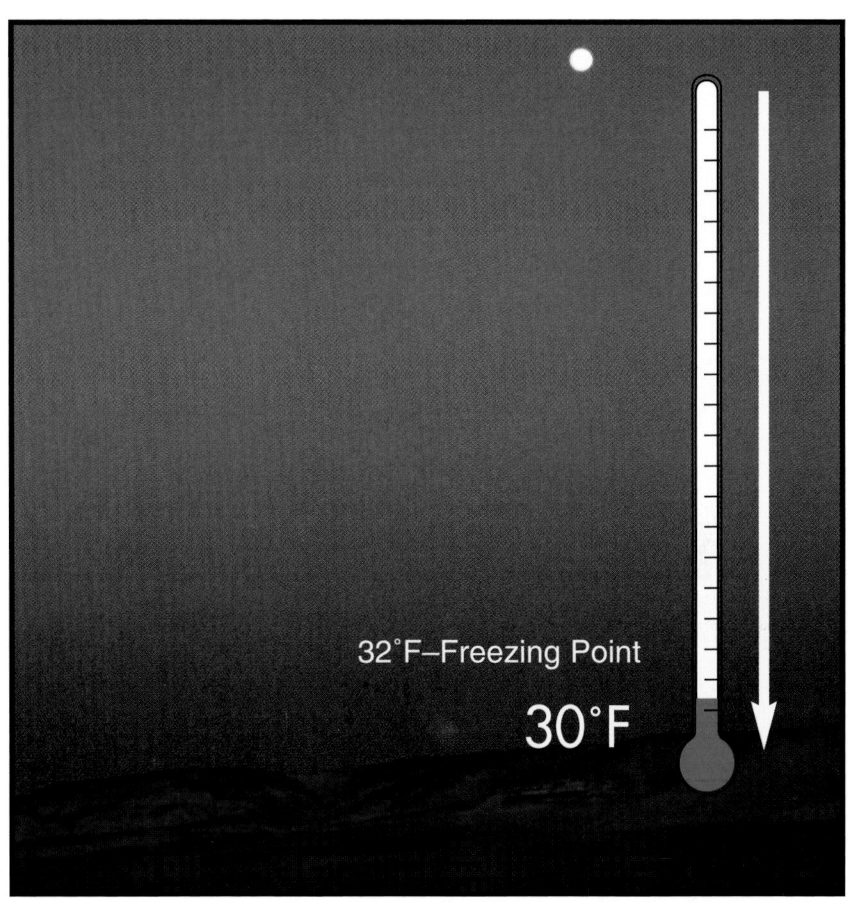

At night, the temperature drops. Some nights the temperature drops to below freezing!

Land

The Sahara has many sand dunes. A sand dune is a mountain of sand. Some dunes can be as high as 600 feet.

That's taller than the Washington Monument.

The Sahara also has mountains. Most of the mountains in the Sahara are in the country of Chad.

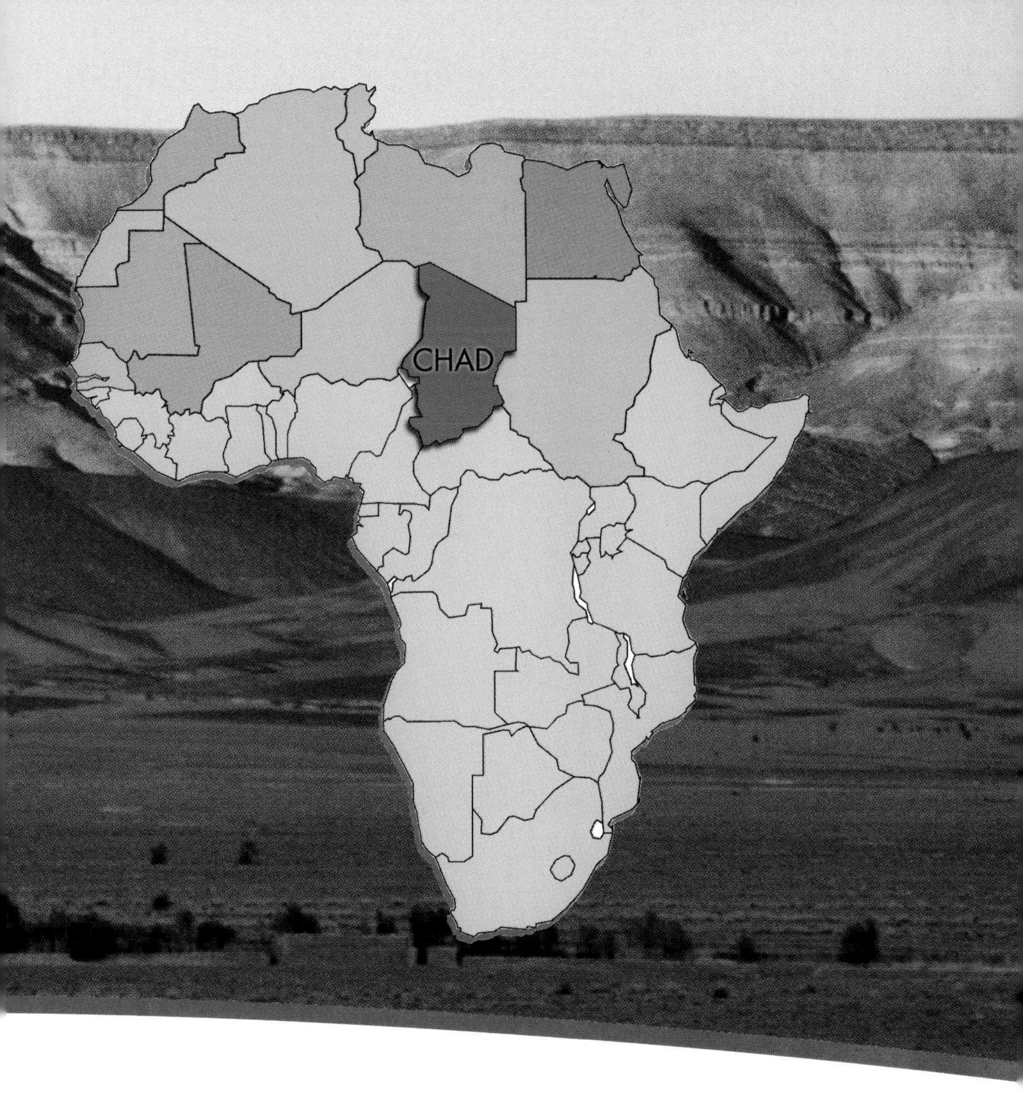

FUN FACT: The highest mountain in the Sahara is Emi Koussi. It is 11,204 feet high. That's as high as eight Empire State Buildings!

People

The Sahara is very large, but not many people live there. The desert has only two and a half million people. That's fewer people than there are in most large cities.

FUN FACT: The United States has more than 275 million people.

An oasis is a part of the desert that has fresh water. There is enough water to grow crops.

People who live in the Sahara usually live near an oasis. It can take days to get from one oasis to another.

The Sahara desert is truly
a natural wonder!

Glossary

desert (**dehz**-ert) a dry, sandy region without water or trees

dunes (**doonz**) mountains of sand

oasis (oh-**ay**-sihs) a place in the desert where there is water and where trees and plants can grow

temperature (**tehm**-puhr-uh-chuhr) how hot or cold something is

Resources

Books

52 Days by Camel: My Sahara Adventure
by Lawrie Raskin
Firefly Books (1998)

The Sahara and Its People
by Simon Scoones
Thomson Learning (1995)

Web Site

http://www.pbs.org/sahara

Index

Word Count: 322

Note to Librarians, Teachers, and Parents

If reading is a challenge, Reading Power is a solution! Reading Power is perfect for readers who want high-interest subject matter at an accessible reading level. These fact-filled, photo-illustrated books are designed for readers who want straightforward vocabulary, engaging topics, and a manageable reading experience. With clear picture/text correspondence, leveled Reading Power books put the reader in charge. Now readers have the power to get the information they want and the skills they need in a user-friendly format.